ideals®
CHRISTMAS

Christmas is here:
merry old Christmas,
gift-bearing, heart-touching,
joy-bringing Christmas,
day of grand memories,
king of the year!

—Washington Irving

ideals®

Nashville, Tennessee

Open Your Heart

Minnie Klemme

Wreathe your home
    with Christmas;
open wide the door.
Let the dear Lord enter;
there is room for more:
room for friend and stranger—
Jesus makes the start.
If the inn is taken,
    open wide your heart.

Christmas

Helen Crawford

The candles are lighted;
the tree is aglow;
the Yule log is blazing,
and outside—the snow!

'Tis Christmas! And yonder
the light of the star
draws closer together
all friends near and far.

Image © Jason/Adobe Stock

Lady Selecting Her Christmas Cards

Phyllis McGinley

Fastidiously, with gloved and careful fingers,
　　Through the marked samples she pursues her search.
Which shall it be: the snowscape's wintry languors
　　Complete with church,

An urban skyline, children sweetly pretty
　　Sledding downhill, the chaste ubiquitous wreath,
Schooner or candle or the simple Scottie
　　With verse underneath?

Perhaps it might be better to emblazon
　　With words alone the stiff, punctilious square.
(Oh, not Victorian, certainly. This season
　　One meets it everywhere.)

She has a duty proper to the weather—
　　A Birth she must announce, a rumor to spread,
Wherefore the very spheres once sang together
　　And a star shone overhead.

Here are the Tidings which the shepherds panted
　　One to another, kneeling by their flocks.
And they will bear her name (engraved, not printed),
　　Twelve-fifty for the box.

Keeping Christmas

Henry van Dyke

It is a good thing to observe Christmas Day. The mere marking of times and seasons, when men agree to stop work and make merry together, is a wise and wholesome custom. It helps one to feel the supremacy of the common life over the individual life. It reminds a man to set his own little watch, now and then, by the great clock of humanity which runs on sun time.

But there is a better thing than the observance of Christmas Day, and that is keeping Christmas.

Are you willing to forget what you have done for other people and to remember what other people have done for you; to ignore what the world owes you and to think what you owe the world; to put your rights in the background and your duties in the middle distance and your chances to do a little more than your duty in the foreground; to see that your fellow men are just as real as you are and try to look behind their faces to their hearts, hungry for joy; to own that probably the only good reason for your existence is not what you are going to get out of life but what you are going to give to life; to close your book of complaints against the management of the universe and look around you for a place where you can sow a few seeds of happiness—are you willing to do these things for even a day? Then you can keep Christmas.

Are you willing to stoop down and consider the needs and desires of little children; to remember the weakness and loneliness of people who are growing old; to stop asking how much your friends love you, and ask yourself whether you love them enough; to bear in mind the things that other people have to bear on their hearts; to try to understand what those who live in the same house with you really want, without waiting for them to tell you; to trim your lamp so that it will give more light and less smoke; and to carry it in front so that your shadow will fall behind you; to make a grave for your ugly thoughts and a garden for your kind feelings with the gate open—are you willing to do these things even for a day? Then you can keep Christmas.

Are you willing to believe that love is the strongest thing in the world—stronger than hate, stronger than death—and that the blessed life which began in Bethlehem nineteen hundred years ago is the image and brightness of Eternal Love? Then you can keep Christmas.

And if you keep it for a day, why not always? But you can never keep it alone.

Home for Christmas

Garnett Ann Schultz

There's a friendly sort of feeling
with the ground so fresh and white,
wreaths of holly in the windows
and the tree all shining bright,
turkey roasting in the oven
and a welcome on the door—
all is well, you're home for Christmas
with the folks that you adore.

There's a pleasant kind of laughter
when at last the work is done,
every present wrapped so lovely
tied with ribbons one by one.
All the house is put in order
for this extra-special day,
and you're glad you're home for Christmas
where each heart is bright and gay.

How you love the little children
as they hurry here and there,
with their little eyes just beaming
as they do their precious share.
Could they be such perfect angels?
Never seemed so good before!
They are pleased you're home for Christmas
and they meet you at the door.

Home for Christmas—nothing like it!—
just the grandest time of all,
with a million dreams to treasure
and a memory to recall,
while the family there about you,
each one in the same old place,
you are home and it is Christmas:
smiles of gladness light each face.

Deck the Halls with Christmas Spirit

Bea Bourgeois

Some people drape a few strands of garland on the mantel, hang a wreath on the front door, and consider their homes decorated for the Christmas season. They would probably be astonished to learn that my husband begins his holiday decorating every year on the day after Thanksgiving and takes at least a week of vacation early in December so that he can merrily deck our halls.

I don't know anyone who enjoys the Christmas season more than Bob does. Decorating is not only a hobby with him; it's a month-long labor of love, and the end result is magnificent. We store dozens of cardboard boxes in the attic, holding carefully wrapped Christmas items that we've collected through the years. There are antique glass ornaments, Christmas postcards, papier-mâché Santas and Father Christmas figures, twirly metal icicles, and tinsel. Once we begin bringing the boxes downstairs, the Christmas spirit comes right along with them.

Each year the top of our upright piano becomes a miniature replica of Bethlehem. Bob covers the top with a wide strip of brown felt, and places the manger in the center. Figures carved from olive wood approach the crib; there are Wise Men and shepherds, and camels in single file, joined by small metal chains to form a procession. A choir of porcelain angels stands to one side.

Perhaps the most ingenious touch—people quite literally gasp in astonishment when they see it—is the Christmas wall Bob designed. He invented the wall because we had run out of space to display all the cards we receive each year, and it has become an annual holiday tradition in our dining room. The background is made of strands of red and green yarn, attached to eye screws on the moldings at the top and bottom of the wall. Bob threads the yarn from bottom to top in alternating colors until it forms hundreds of diamond-shaped pockets. Each individual diamond is tied with a short piece of yarn to provide enough tension so that decorations can be hung.

It takes a full day to string the yarn onto the wall, and one evening to tie all the diamonds, with everybody in the family sharing the job. Then the fun begins. Boxes are opened and trinkets unwrapped; the wall features delightful holiday items our sons made during their grade-school years, miniature brass musical instruments, Victorian slipper ornaments, and hundreds of small stuffed animals—including a marvelous felt mouse dressed in the red and white robes of a cardinal and named, appropriately, "Church Mouse." There are felt soldier boys and teddy bears, giraffes and gingerbread boys, and tiny handmade sleighs and stars. When all the decorations are hung, we add the Christmas cards by hanging them on strands of red and green yarn.

The window seat in our dining room is transformed each holiday season into a winter village, complete with a miniature church, several small buildings, and a mirrored "skating pond." Bob and the boys set up part of our old electric train set on a piece of plywood covered with green carpet tiles. The tracks run along the outside edge of the board, and "snow" (from a box of Ivory Flakes) is sprinkled on the entire scene.

There is a lighted station house, a miniature goose on the "pond," a duck standing imperiously in the town square, and a hand-crocheted schoolhouse that was made by a friend especially for the tableau. The train chugs through the winter night, complete with crossing gates that raise and lower and a stop at the barrel factory in the corner. Young visitors are absolutely fascinated with the old lighted Pullman cars and the stern station master who raises and lowers his arm as the train chugs past.

Our sons have become steeped in holiday traditions, particularly where the Christmas tree is concerned; they are appalled at the thought of buying an artificial tree. Every year our tree stands a majestic eight or nine feet tall, and it is dressed most elegantly in garland, strings of popcorn, and hundreds of ornaments, mostly antique. Every year Bob puts on the lights and the boys hang the ornaments; we sip eggnog and listen to Christmas carol records, and we dare not deviate from this well-established routine.

The outside of our house looks almost as pretty as the inside during the month of December. Bob and the boys have strung hundreds of miniature white lights on a stately cedar tree in our front yard, and the cherry tree in the backyard wears

Image © teressa/Adobe Stock

several strings of large colored lights. In each window there are electric candelabras with three candles apiece; on a dark winter night the house looks as though it belongs in a small Austrian village. On the front porch, Bob hangs a huge three-foot round wreath that he made several years ago out of pinecones and nuts.

Friends look forward to a holiday visit so they can admire the painstaking detail and the beautiful decorations that make our house a December delight. When they marvel at the amount of patience it all takes, Bob smiles and says, simply, "I just love Christmas."

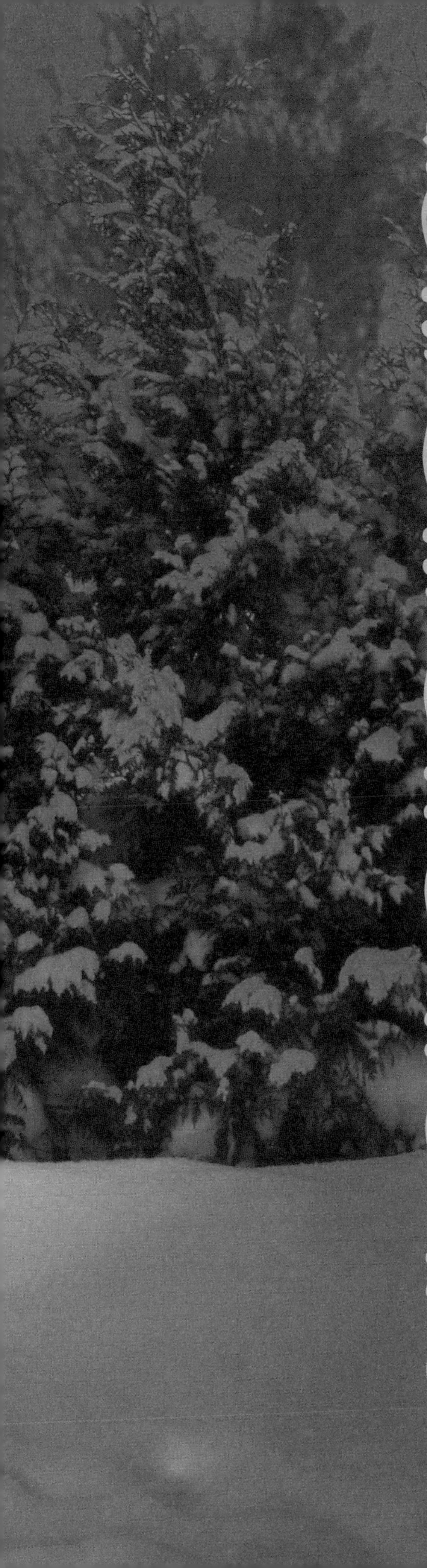

A Tree of Christmas

Marguerite Gode

Grew a little pine tree
on a high hill,
the moon was silver,
the wind was still;
came a snow fairy
in a robe of white,
spied the little fir tree,
chortled with delight.

One by one the branches
turned to gleaming strands,
touched by misty magic
of the fairy's hands;
stars fell to dangle,
moonbeams spread about,
as the little pine tree
gaily blossomed out.

Birds sang a carol,
sleigh bells chimed a song,
frost maidens curtsied,
as they danced along;
grew a little pine tree
from a forest wild,
to a tree of Christmas
for a fairy child.

Image © Lloret/iStock

Snow
Dorothy Aldis

The fence posts wear
    marshmallow hats
on a snowy day;
bushes in their nightgowns
are kneeling down to pray—
and all the trees have silver skirts
and want to dance away.

The Little Red Sled
Jocelyn Bush

"Come out with me!"
    cried the little red sled.
"I'll give you the wings
    of a bird," it said.
"The ground is all snowy;
the wind is all blowy!
We'll go like a fairy,
so light and so airy!"

Snow in the City
Rachel Field

Snow is out of fashion,
but it still comes down
to whiten all the buildings
in our town;
to dull the noise of traffic;
to dim each glaring light
with star-shaped feathers
of frosty white.
And not the tallest building,
halfway up the sky;
or all the trains
   and buses
and taxis scudding by;
and not a million people,
not one of them at all,
can do a thing about
   the snow
but let it fall!

Christmas Eve: Nearing Midnight in New York
Langston Hughes

The Christmas trees are almost all sold,
and the ones that are left go cheap;
The children almost all over town
have almost gone to sleep.

The skyscraper lights on
   Christmas Eve
have almost all gone out.
There's very little traffic,
almost no one about.

Our town's almost as quiet
as Bethlehem must have been
before a sudden angel chorus
sang PEACE ON EARTH!
GOOD WILL TO MEN!

Our old Statue of Liberty
looks down almost with a smile
as the Island of Manhattan
awaits the morning of the Child.

New York City's Gapstow Bridge. Image © f11photo/Adobe Stock

The Light Fantastic

Anne Kennedy Brady

When I was a kid, one of my favorite traditions was driving around the neighborhood to see Christmas lights. There were the simple houses, with strings of white lights outlining the roof and windows. There were more festive houses, with colored lights venturing down the walkway and maybe even wrapped around some trees and bushes in the yard. Then there were the houses that were "a little much." This category included anything that moved, blinked, and extended beyond the existing structures. A jolly illuminated snowman? Eight tiny reindeer atop your bungalow? "It's a little much," my parents would comment. And I agreed. As my brothers repeatedly insisted, in their too-cool, teenage effort to end our trip early (but I earnestly believed them): Our house was the best one.

When my husband and I purchased a lovely "duplex down" after the birth of our first child, I was especially delighted with its long, narrow, covered front deck. After years of rented apartments with limiting rules around decor, here was our very own outdoor space to do with as we pleased! I bought three boxes of colored lights as soon as we signed the purchase papers.

One chilly Saturday early in December while baby Milo napped, Kevin and I strung lights along the railing of our porch. I suggested it would be nice to hang lights from the overhang as well, so Kevin made the trip to pick up a few more boxes. He returned with a snowman.

"Frosty" seemed awfully close to "a little much," but with his jaunty scarf and stuffed carrot nose, I had to admit he was pretty cute. I put him together while Kevin tried to maneuver the lights up the metal post in the center of our deck. (We were forced to resort to duct tape.) Frosty, meanwhile, swayed happily in the December breeze, firmly zip-tied into place. That evening, when we flipped the lights on, Milo stared enchanted at the bulbous white figure and clapped his chubby hands. There was no going back.

From there, things got a little out of hand. The next year, we doubled the lights. Another year, an early winter windstorm divested poor Frosty of his scarf, one arm, and his ability to stand upright. Kevin took another trip to the big-box store to buy a replacement and returned with not only a bigger (and inexplicably gold) snowman, but also a trumpeting angel "to balance him out!" The next year, two birds joined the menagerie at my request. Then, having run out of room on the deck, we bought an additional string of lights and illuminated the fire escape stairs too. At one point, I lamented that icicle lights were no longer around—a trend from the 1990s wherein multiple short strands hung from one longer strand, resembling delicate icicles but in fact posing a major fire hazard. So Kevin found an updated LED set I can only describe as "stalactite chic." This string of ten-inch plastic stakes glowed neon versions of Christmas colors, and blinked slowly, blinked quickly, or "shimmered," all with the touch of a button on a remote control that we had to hide from the children almost immediately.

Last year, as we stood across the street admiring our efforts, I began to worry if this was "a little much." Despite having long since vetoed the icicles, the overall effect was not dissimilar to a discotheque. Colored lights of varying brightness surrounded a ragtag lineup of winter-adjacent creatures. Some were even (gasp!) "shimmering." I made a mental note to cancel my order for a bespectacled penguin. "Maybe we went overboard," I suggested meekly. "No way!" Kevin said, grinning. I was doubtful.

Then, the following Friday evening, I was driving both kids home from a late swim lesson. To pass the time, we pointed out the Christmas lights that had popped up since the week before. "That one is only red and green!" Milo shouted. "That one looks like a princess castle!" breathed his four-year-old sister, Helen. And as I fretted over each neighbor's choices (Better? Classier?) we turned the corner onto our street. Before I even registered the glow from our uneven light fantastic, Helen squealed, "Look! There's OUR house! I LOVE our house!" And Milo, in his mildly bored tone I find overly confident for a seven-year-old, stated, "Yeah, it's the best one."

I couldn't hold back a laugh. I stopped the car and we took a moment to admire our handiwork. Both kids oohed and aahed over the creatures, the lights, the memories of helping Dad unpack everything. Our house isn't exactly understated, and it's not way over-the-top, but honestly, it wouldn't matter if it was. Our house is warm and welcoming. It's colorful and festive. It doesn't always match—it reflects who we are, and it changes as we change. And yes, it might be "a little much." But it's definitely the best one.

Christmas decorations in Brooklyn, New York.
Image © Oksana Byelikova/Dreamstime.com

Family Recipes

Cinnamon Cream-Cheese Bars

3   tablespoons butter
½   cup brown sugar
2   eggs, divided
1   teaspoon ground cinnamon
    Pinch of kosher salt

2   8-ounce cans refrigerated crescent rolls
2   8-ounce packages cream cheese, softened
½   cup granulated sugar, plus additional for topping
1   teaspoon vanilla extract

Preheat oven to 350°F. In a small saucepan over medium-low heat, melt butter. Add brown sugar and cook until sugar and butter are well combined, about 3 minutes. Remove from heat and allow to cool about 10 minutes. Whisk in 1 egg, cinnamon, and salt. Set aside. In a greased 9 x 13-inch casserole dish, roll out 1 can of crescent roll dough, pressing seams together to form a crust. In a large bowl, beat cream cheese, 1 egg, sugar, and vanilla until well combined. Spread evenly over the crust.

Pour cinnamon filling over the cream-cheese mixture and spread evenly. On a large sheet of waxed paper, roll out remaining can of crescent roll dough, forming a 9 x 13-inch rectangle, pressing the seams together. Carefully invert dough over filling to form a top crust. Bake 30 minutes, until top crust is golden. Remove from the oven and dust with additional sugar. Cut into 1½ to 2-inch squares. Serve warm or at room temperature. Makes 20 to 24 bars.

Chocolate Scotcheroos

1   cup light corn syrup
1   cup granulated sugar
1   cup peanut butter

6   cups crispy rice cereal
1   cup semisweet chocolate chips
1   cup butterscotch chips

In a medium saucepan over medium heat, combine corn syrup and sugar. Cook, stirring frequently, until sugar dissolves and mixture begins to boil. Remove from heat and stir in peanut butter until well combined. Add rice cereal and stir until well coated. Press mixture into a greased 9 x 13-inch baking dish. In a small saucepan over low heat, melt chocolate and butterscotch chips, stirring constantly. Spread evenly over cereal mixture. Let stand until firm, about 20 minutes. Cut into 1½ to 2-inch squares. Makes 20 to 24 Scotcheroos.

Pecan Pie Bars

3 cups all-purpose flour
1½ cups granulated sugar, divided
½ teaspoon salt
1 cup butter
1½ cups light corn syrup

½ cup brown sugar
4 eggs
3 tablespoons butter, melted
1½ teaspoons vanilla extract
2½ cups chopped pecans

Preheat oven to 350°F. In a large bowl, combine flour, ½ cup sugar, and salt. Cut in 1 cup butter until mixture resembles coarse crumbs. In a parchment-paper-lined 10 x 15-inch jelly-roll pan, sprinkle the mixture evenly; press in firmly. Bake 20 minutes. Meanwhile, in a large bowl, mix corn syrup, 1 cup sugar, brown sugar, eggs, 3 tablespoons melted butter, and vanilla until smooth. Stir in pecans. Spread filling evenly over baked crust as soon as it comes out of the oven. Return to oven and bake until filling is mostly set, about 25 to 30 minutes. Cool completely in pan on a wire rack before slicing into 2½-inch bars. Makes 24 bars.

Chai-Spiced Pumpkin Bars

½ cup old-fashioned rolled oats
½ cup pumpkin seeds
½ cup unsweetened shredded coconut
2 teaspoons ground cinnamon, divided
⅜ teaspoon salt, divided
1 to 1⅓ cups chopped pitted dates
1½ cups pumpkin puree
⅓ cup maple syrup

¼ cup coconut oil, melted
1 teaspoon vanilla extract
¾ teaspoon cardamom
¾ teaspoon ground ginger
¼ teaspoon ground cloves
⅛ teaspoon black pepper
2 tablespoons coconut flour

In a food processor, pulse oats, pumpkin seeds, coconut, ½ teaspoon cinnamon, and ⅛ teaspoon salt until finely ground. Add ⅔ cup dates and process until well combined and sticky. The mixture may look crumbly, but it should hold together when pinched between your fingers. If necessary, add more dates to get the right consistency. Press dough evenly into an 8 x 8-inch parchment-paper-lined baking pan. Place in freezer. In a food processor, combine pumpkin puree, maple syrup, coconut oil, vanilla, ¼ teaspoon salt, 1½ teaspoons cinnamon, and remaining spices; blend until smooth. Add coconut flour and blend until well combined. Remove crust from freezer and spread filling evenly on top. Cover and refrigerate at least 6 hours or overnight.

Lift bars out of pan using parchment paper edges. Cut into 12 pieces, wiping the knife clean between cuts. Serve chilled. Makes 12 bars.

Seek and Ye Shall Find

Michele Christian

My family has a little pre-Christmas tradition that has gone on for years. It's the thrill of the hunt, the victory of the find—peeking before Christmas! We have complete and utter defiance for the "Do Not Open Until Christmas" tags on gifts.

One Christmas, my dad bought my mom a wooden rocking chair. She had hounded him all year for a solid oak chair with a cushioned seat for the corner of the living room. He found exactly the one she had described, wrapped it ever-so-carefully, and tucked the wrapped box under the tree. One day, as he was putting other gifts under the tree, he noticed a small tear in the front of the box. The hole appeared to be about the size of a finger poke. The next day he noticed the hole was a little longer, and the day after that it was even longer! My dad knew not to ask if my mom was snooping, though. She'd never admit it. But when it comes to my mother, really, why bother wrapping? She must have figured out what it was at some point, because the hole didn't get any bigger.

I can't help it, either; I suppose the temptation is too great. But I can just smile and say, "Well, Mom does it!" if I ever get caught.

One day, I was at my uncle's house when he had just returned from holiday shopping. He walked briskly past me, on a mission to hide gifts in his bedroom before anyone saw. He came out quickly, shutting the door behind him, and headed to the kitchen.

What was in there? I had to know. I approached the bedroom door, opened it slowly, and peeked in. On the bed were brand-new winter coats for everyone! Oh, what to do, what to do? I had to tell someone. Someone who would understand the pleasure of my discovery and savor this experience . . . my mother!

I sneaked into the living room and told her what I had seen. At first, she scolded me: "You're not supposed to be looking in there!" But she couldn't help adding, "But tell me what you saw."

One year, though, my brothers crossed the line. Mark was twelve and Jim was eleven. They wanted a new video game system for Christmas, in the worst way. One day, while my parents were out, their curiosity got the best of them. They began searching the house top to bottom, like a couple of wild animals on the hunt. Mark scoured the attic, and Jim rummaged through closets. Finally, they found it—a brand-new Nintendo system sitting on the top shelf in my mother's bedroom closet! They didn't stop there. They yanked the box off the shelf and stared wildly at it, in awe that they were really getting what they'd wanted for Christmas! During their celebration, Jim looked over and noticed a camera on my dad's nightstand. He turned on the camera, pointed it at Mark, and said, "Hey, Mark, hold up the box. Say cheese!" Mark grinned widely, evidence in hand, as Jim snapped the scandalous picture. Then Jim returned the camera to the nightstand. They placed the box where they'd found it in the closet and ran outside to play.

It was a week before Christmas, and my brothers and I came home from school to find my parents sitting at the kitchen table with an envelope of newly developed photos. Mark and Jim went pale. Both started to giggle nervously and couldn't stop. They suddenly remembered their adventure from the prior week and realized they'd been caught. My dad had a serious look on his face as he pulled the pictures out of the envelope. The picture on the top of the stack was the incriminating photo showing Mark holding the Nintendo system, sporting a smile full of braces.

My dad let out a loud sigh and began, "So I picked up some pictures today . . ." but he started laughing so hard that he couldn't finish the sentence. Finally, catching his breath and clearing his throat, he said, "What were you two thinking? Were you hoping I wasn't going to develop these until after Christmas?" and laughed some more.

My brothers had no answer, except for

Image © SuperStock/Blend Images

shrugging their shoulders and mumbling. Mark and Jim were fortunate to still get the Nintendo for Christmas—my family understands the curse of temptation. They were grounded, however, for going through Mom's closet.

When my dad finished laying out their punishment, he turned to all of us and said nonchalantly, "Oh, by the way, thanks for the drill—it's just what I wanted. I promise to act surprised when I open it on Christmas." Then he casually walked out of the room, laughing the whole way.

Bundles

John Farrar

A bundle is a funny thing,
it always sets me wondering;
for whether it is thin or wide,
you never know just what's inside.

Especially on Christmas week,
temptation is so great to peek!
Now wouldn't it be much more fun
if shoppers carried things undone?

Moral Injunctions

Helen C. Smith

'Twas a month
    before Christmas,
every cranny and nook
bore the moral injunction:
"Don't you peek,
    don't you look!"
If you wanted your cap
or some warm underwear,
and got down
    on your knees,
or climbed up on a chair
to look for the thing,

you would hear
    someone say:
"Now you quit
    your snooping—
you go right away!"

Tom, caught
    in the pantry,
"looking for skates,"
was prying the
    lid off a
carton of dates!

Mary, "looking
    for scissors
to cut off a thread,"
was caught
    on her knees
looking under the bed!

So Grandma
    (God bless her!)
goes slyly about . . .
detecting the peepers
and driving them out!

Sing a Song of Christmas Carols

Marjorie Holmes

"Deck the halls with boughs of holly" . . . and wash the curtains and polish the silver. And clean out the fireplace and haul in the wood. And try to find the old tree base. And dig out those cartons of decorations to see how many are good for another year.

"While shepherds watched their flocks by night" . . . sit up late making doll clothes. And finishing a sweater and painting a sled. And helping your husband uncrate a bicycle. And then steal around, checking on your own flock, before collapsing into bed.

"Good Christian men, rejoice" . . . when the last box is finally wrapped and tied and in the mail, and you're at least halfway through addressing the greeting cards.

"We three kings of Orient are, bearing gifts we traverse afar" . . . to church and parties and school bazaars. And shut-ins and hospitals and children's homes. And that family whose mother is ill and whose father is out of a job.

"O come, all ye faithful, joyful and triumphant" . . . that somehow it's all done! The church bells are ringing, it's time to come—come, children and neighbors and aunts and uncles and cousins. . . . Come and behold Him. "O come, let us adore Him!"

"Away in a manger, no crib for a bed" . . . a three-year-old is curled up in a pew, fast asleep.

"It came upon the midnight clear" . . . that little voice calling out:

"Is it morning yet? Did Santa Claus come?"

"Silent night, holy night, all is calm, all is bright" . . . at last. It is, it truly is. "Sleep in heavenly peace."

"Hark! the herald angels sing" . . . at the crack of dawn, "Get up, get up, Merry Christmas!"

"Joy to the world . . . Let earth receive her King" . . . and people their gifts, and parents their hugs. . . . Let children run back and forth to each other's houses, and neighbors pop in for a cup of wassail and to admire the shining tree. . . . Let heaven and nature and your own heart sing!

"God rest you merry, gentlemen" . . . and women. "Let nothing you dismay!"

Even though the whole house is an explosion of candy, nuts, papers, presents, and ribbon; the tags are so mixed up nobody knows who to thank for what; and the cat is knocking ornaments off the tree.

Add another log to the fire snapping so fragrant on the grate, baste the turkey already golden in the oven. Fling open the door to grandparents and other guests who come tramping up the snowy walk. With true love and brotherhood, each other now embrace.

God rest you merry, mothers and fathers and families and friends, at the end of this glorious Christmas Day!

Christmas Morning

Elsie Melchert Fowler

This is the magic morning—
tumble out of bed,
tiptoe down the long stairs
softly on each tread.
Oh, what's this before you?
Rub your sleepy eyes—
golden lights and silver,
beautiful surprise!
Sparkling tree of wonder,
gifts, enchanting, new—
magic, magic morning,
Christmas dream come true!

The Christmas Tree

Fritz Peters

Deep in the winter night, the family will come one by one, carrying great and small boxes, brilliant in all colors, ribboned in red and green, silver and gold, bright blue, placing them under me with the hands of their hearts, until all around me they are piled high, climbing up into my branches, spilling over onto the floor about me. In the early morning, with all my candles burning and all my brilliant colors standing out and twinkling in their light, the children in their pajamas and woolen slippers rub their sleeping eyes and stare at me in amazement. The mother with her hair hanging down her back smiles and glances here and there, and the father looks up and down at me, quiet and pleased . . . for I am the Christmas tree.

An *Ideals* Christmas

Andrew L. Luna

Next to the Sears Christmas Wish Book catalog that would come to our home every October, the one thing I anxiously anticipated coming in the mail was our annual issue of *Christmas Ideals*. While I looked forward to all of their seasonal and holiday editions, the Christmas issues evoke some of my fondest memories.

My mom used the magazine as a supplement to teach me how to read when I was younger. I remember snuggling up to her in our living room by the tree while the incandescent sounds of Nat King Cole's Christmas album played in the background. We would first look at the many beautiful pictures, and Mom would inevitably comment on a decoration pictured that she would like to make. I loved the way the heavy parchment of the pages felt in my hand and how the covers always popped with color.

Some of my favorite artwork came from the classical, German-influenced work of George Hinke. His Santa paintings, particularly the one where Saint Nick is observing glass Christmas ornaments being made by his elves, were so intricate and lifelike. His depictions of the Nativity were so intimate and personal that I always felt a connection to the Baby Jesus as Mom held me close to her.

I would enjoy Mom reading the poems, essays, and scriptures to me from the richly colored and sometimes foil- or glitter-infused paper. Mom would then have me try my hand at reading a favorite passage and, upon completion,

we would reward ourselves with cold milk and warm seven-layer Christmas cookies. Afterward, we continued to observe the pictures of snow-covered houses and byways as well as the happy pictures of kittens and puppies posed beside Christmas trees and colorfully wrapped presents.

As I grew older, I still loved sitting in the living room alone or with Mom to read the works of Edgar A. Guest, Eugene Field, and Hal Borland. In fact, it was Borland's style and Mom's encouragement that turned me on to being a writer. As

Painting by George Hinke. Image © Ideals/Hachette Book Group

I got older, each new Christmas edition of *Ideals* had a special meaning to me.

In 1975, the cover was red, depicting a nativity set. That was the year I got my license and I looked forward to taking my dad's car around town to look at the wonderful Christmas decorations. In 1977, the scene was people in a snow-covered town heading toward church. That would be the year I graduated from high school and would have to start making more of my own decisions. One of the most memorable covers was back in 1982.

It was red with white poinsettias and candles in the center. That was the year I asked my wife to marry me.

What started as a whimsical idea back in 1944 by Van B. Hooper, a Milwaukee public relations manager, has endured as a reminder of the spirit and warmth of Christmas for many families. Upon getting my new edition of *Ideals* each year, my thoughts quickly drift back to loving hugs, warm cookies, and pleasant times with my mom and family during Christmastime.

80
YEARS *of* IDEALS

A Christmas Tradition

In 1944, the first edition of *Ideals* was published, a Christmas issue printed by Van B. Hooper, a public relations manager for a Milwaukee, Wisconsin, manufacturer. The magazine, which had started as bits and pieces of poetry and homey philosophy added to his company's newsletter, struck a chord with readers.

Hooper described it as "a book of old-fashioned ideals, homey philosophy, poetry, music, inspiration, and art—things some of us may have overlooked during these busy days." The first *Ideals* issue ran as a limited edition due to the severe paper shortage during the war. Circulation grew through word of mouth, and at the magazine's height, eight issues a year were published with various themes. The Christmas issues have been the most popular, a Christmastime tradition in countless homes for decades.

Below are selected covers from throughout the history of *Ideals*. The following seven pages are recreated to appear as they did in earlier issues. As this special section illustrates, times have changed. But what have not changed, and what *Ideals* has celebrated for eighty years, are the timeless values and pure joys of Christmas.

1944   1948   1951   1961

1977   1986   1995   2013

Christmas

ideals

(First edition, December, 1944)

edited and prepared
by van b. hooper

★

As the name implies — a book of old fashioned
Christmas ideals — homey philosophy — poetry —
music — inspiration and art.

This is the first of a series of IDEALS books to be
published about every sixty days — others will in-
clude American Ideals, Patriotic Ideals, Historic
Ideals, Thanksgiving Ideals, etc.

Price $1.00 per copy — $3.75 for four different
volumes, $5.50 for six different volumes, or
$10 for twelve different volumes—to be delivered
as published.

Circulation of initial volumes will be very limited, due to
present government restrictions on paper.

★

IDEALS PUBLISHING CO.
MILWAULKEE 1, WIS.

★

★

God Gave Us

God gave us hills,
    white hills in the moonlight,
And lacy gray shadows
    that quiver and run;
And light, fluffy snowflakes
    that sift in the dusk-light,
To a world veiled in stillness
    as the night is begun.

God gave us waters,
    ice-bound and frozen;
God gave us little white
    tracks in the snow;
And little fat sparrows
    that sleep in the church-tops,
And bells that peal out
    to the stillness below.

God gave us Christmas
    and bright wreaths of holly;
Taught us, like Jesus,
    to bless and forgive;
Tilled all our hearts
    with that peace universal;
And God gave us love
    and the spirit to give.

Our sincere thanks
to the unknown author.

Country
CHRONICLE

Lansing Christman

I do not mind that December opens the windows of the year to another wintertime. Despite the wind and cold, the rain and sleet and snow, December brings a spark of love and faith, for the Christmas season is then at hand.

I still find the joy and exuberance I knew as a child. Living in the country all these years has kept me close to the joy of the Yuletide, the real meaning of Christmas, and the hope and trust that come to one whose faith is based on the birth of the Christ Child in Bethlehem.

I carry in from the woods an evergreen that will stand in the corner of a room. I decorate the tree with sparkling ornaments of red, green, gold, silver, and blue. The colors gleam in the brilliance of a lighted room.

From the woods, I gather ground pine to add its green to the overall atmosphere of the season. From the swamps, I collect black alder twigs loaded with their clusters of brilliant red berries to be placed on the mantel over the fireplace and in small vases around the room.

The countryside is covered in a blanket of pristine white. It shines like diamonds in the winter sun and glows and sparkles when touched by the light of the stars high in the heavens.

Bells and carols spread love and joy and add to the true spirit of Christmastime. As the birds visit the feeders outside my door, I hear this holy season of love in the songs they sing.

I need no other gifts as long as I have my loving friendships and the beauty and songs around me. I meditate and dream, for the memories of many Christmastimes continue to point the way to the birth of our Savior who promised eternal life for those who believe—and so I believe.

R. A. Johnson

CHRISTMAS TREE TOWN

NOT INCORPORATED
POP. SANTA CLAUS AND HIS 10,000 HELPERS

NORTH POLE — JUST OVER THE HILL

SOUTH POLE — 25,002 MILES

● *Karen Lee*

It's hustle and bustle
In Christmas-Tree Town,
With bright little sleighs
Rushing uphill and down,
And plump little drivers
That whistle and shout,
As they hurry and scurry
And tumble about.

Their sharp little axes
Go chippery-chop,
As deep in the forest
The little trees drop.
Then off to the workshop
Where elves are at play,
Retrimming the branches
To make them more gay.

It's see-saw and tick-tack
And wind in and out
Bright ribbons of rainbows
With stars strung about.
It's climb up and fall down
And hammer your thumb.
It's yodel and carol
And whistle and hum.

These gay little creatures
The whole season thru
Are plotting and planning
A present for you—
From deep in the forest
A pine tree so gay
It will lighten and brighten
Your whole Christmas Day.

These Precious Gifts

Letitia Morse Nash

Long years ago the Magi came
With gifts of precious things,
And laid them at the tiny feet
Of Jesus, King of kings.

Oh, may we give such precious gifts
From out our heart's rich store . . .
That Christmas Day shall come to be
A blessing, more and more.

The world has need of all our love,
And smiling service sweet . . .
So may we bring these precious gifts
To lay them at His feet.

Christmas Is the Miracle
Alice Mackenzie Swaim

Down the years of memory,
the pageant of Decembers,
Christmas is the miracle
that every heart remembers.

Above the dreaming
little towns,
the fields of drifted snow,

there falls the benediction
of the Christmas star's
warm glow.

And heavy hearts grow lighter,
and joyful voices ring,
to celebrate His birthday
and worship Christ, the King.

Christmas Is Remembering
Charles R. Isley

Christmas is remembering
the jewel-studded trees;
the singing of the carolers
brings happy memories.

The family get-togethers,
the revelry and fun
of hanging decorations,
the stockings neatly hung.

Old customs from far places
commingled with our own
create a new tradition,
the greatest ever known.

And as the gifts are given,
our grateful hearts recall
the Christ Child in a manger . . .
most precious gift of all!

HOLIDAY EXPRESS *by Mary Ann Vessey. Image © Mary Ann Vessey*

Through My Window

A Perfectly Imperfect Christmas

Pamela Kennedy

Years ago, when we lived in Hawaii, a friend introduced me to a fascinating Japanese art form called *Kintsugi*. In Kintsugi, one repairs a broken piece of pottery by gluing the pieces back together with a special lacquer dusted or mixed with powdered gold. When the piece is thus reconstructed, the broken places become marks of beauty. Instead of hiding the cracks, they are highlighted, and the newly restored piece is "perfectly imperfect."

This art form took on a new meaning for me last Christmas when my perfectly planned holiday was shattered by circumstances beyond my control. As usual, I had begun preparations well in advance. I had shopped for gifts, planned the menus, and decorated the beach house with the usual holiday decor. I even added a few new touches—I framed the doorway to the kids' room with tiny red and green lights and dubbed it "The Elves' Den." All that remained was for my husband and me to wrap all the gifts and deposit them under the tree. Then we would wait for our adult kids and the grandkids to arrive for a three-day post-Christmas celebration on New Year's weekend.

What we hadn't planned was that I would receive unexpected medical news the week before Christmas and would require two major neck surgeries within 2 weeks! There would be no family gathering with beautifully wrapped gifts. No sitting in front of a blazing fire with grandchildren dressed in matching Christmas jammies. No making of homemade cinnamon rolls with my daughter in town from Chicago. No tantalizing aromas of roasted beef wafting through the house. No watching the children rip into carefully chosen Christmas gifts. My perfectly planned Christmas was in shards.

There were more serious concerns, to be sure. But still, I grieved the loss of these once-a-year moments. I longed to see our young families enjoying time together, having good conversations, and watching their children get reacquainted after almost a year apart. As I lay in my hospital bed, I looked at the broken pieces of my Christmas plans and tried to figure out a way to reconstruct them. My husband, far more practical than I, offered, "We can give them their gifts in March or April or whenever. It just doesn't matter!" He wasn't wrong, but I wasn't quite ready to go along with it. Maybe there was a way . . .

Recuperating at home, and probably somewhat influenced by prescription painkillers, I insisted my husband go to the local discount department store and buy ten of the largest Christmas gift bags he could find. He returned

with bags that could hold, literally, a small child (we know this because our granddaughters, ages 8 and 4, each got into one). While all my Christmas gifts were at the beach cabin, I had made a list of what gifts were for each person and saved it on my computer. Dispensing with our usual elaborate gift wrap, I asked my daughter and daughter-in-law to take my list and put each person's gifts into one big bag—forget the fancy paper, the boxes, the ribbons; don't worry about price tags or factory wrapping. Each person would get one child-sized bag holding all their gifts from my husband and me. Oh, and please snag a photo of the grandkids in their matching PJs! To their credit, these loving young women followed my directions to the letter.

On New Year's Eve, my husband and I connected online with our family as they enjoyed opening their gifts from us. It was good medicine seeing them delighted with the things I had chosen over the past months and hearing their joy and excitement. We laughed and even shed a few tears together and when we said, "good night," and turned off the computer, my husband and I both commented on how much fun it was. "And do you realize how much less work it was? And how much less trash we produced?" Later, my son and daughter shared stories of a cousins' beach walk orchestrated by the dads, a pizza dinner (for Christmas!), and several unexpected moments of hilarity, connection, and support. It was an unusual Christmas for sure. Our carefully treasured traditions had been broken apart. But we looked for new ways to celebrate. And as we embraced a different way of doing things, giving thanks for the blessings of answered prayers and healing, I thought of Kintsugi. How beautiful these broken places turned out to be when we put them back together with love. How surprising that our once-shattered Christmas had become, in fact, perfectly imperfect.

Don't Waste the Miracle

Jan Miller Girando

There's a miracle in Christmas—
there's a stillness in the air
and excitement in the shining eyes
of children everywhere.

There's a miracle in Christmas
as each silent night unfolds,
and we see again the promise
that this holy season holds.

There's a wonder in traditions,
in the stories passed along,
in our thoughtfulness toward others,
and in voices raised in song.

There's a reassuring comfort
in the joy glad tidings bring
and an inner peace from honoring
and praising Christ the King.

There's a magic in the season,
in the kindnesses we do,
whether joys are shared by many
or among a special few.

There's awareness of our gratitude
for blessings from above;
there's a miracle in Christmas—
and the miracle is love.

Christmas Is for Giving

Iris W. Bray

Christmas is for giving
and for showing that we care,
for honoring the Christ Child
with the loving gifts we share.
The Wise Men gave of riches;
the shepherds, faith and love.
Each gift, in its own measure,
was smiled on from above.
Let every gift be treasured;
not always size or price
determines the extent of love
and willing sacrifice.
Handsome gifts with festive trim
bring smiles of sweet content,
but modest gifts of humble means
are ofttimes heaven-sent.
Whether it be large or small,
each gift will share in part
the message of true Christmas joy
if given from the heart!

Why It Is

Author Unknown

Though the presents are shiny and the
    paper is bright,
and it is hard to wait through the long
    and cold night
to open them all the very next day
and bring out the wonderful new toys to play . . .
it is important that we all remember
why it is we give gifts at the end of December,
why it is we all gather and joyously sing:
to celebrate the birth of our Savior and King.

Bits & Pieces

Holly and holiness
come well together,
Christ Child and
Santa Claus
share the white weather;
plums in plum pudding and
turkey with dressing,
choirs singing carols—
all have his blessing.
—*Ralph W. Seager*

To cherish peace and
goodwill, to be plenteous
in mercy, is to have the
real spirit of Christmas.
—*Calvin Coolidge*

The merry Christmas, with its
generous boards,
its fire-lit hearths, and gifts and blazing trees,
its pleasant voices uttering gentle words,
its genial mirth, attuned to sweet accords,
its holiest memories!
The fairest season of the passing year—
the merry, merry Christmastime is here.
—*George Arnold*

Christmas is a bridge. We need bridges
as the river of time flows past. Today's
Christmas should mean creating happy hours
for tomorrow and reliving those of yesterday.
—*Gladys Taber*

Christmas,
children, is not
a date. It is a
state of mind.
—*Mary Ellen Chase*

Christmas waves a
magic wand over this
world, and behold,
everything is softer
and more beautiful.
—*Norman Vincent Peale*

What is Christmas?
It is tenderness for the past,
courage for the present,
hope for the future. It is a
wish that every cup may
overflow with blessings rich
and eternal and that every
path may lead to peace.
—*Agnes M. Pharo*

We shall find peace.
We shall hear the angels,
we shall see the sky
sparkling with diamonds.
—*Anton Chekhov*

That Holy Thing

George MacDonald

They all were looking for a king
to slay their foes and lift them high:
Thou cam'st, a little baby thing
that made a woman cry.

O Son of Man, to right my lot
naught but Thy presence can avail;
yet on the road Thy wheels are not,
nor on the sea Thy sail!

My how or when Thou wilt not heed,
but come down Thine own
    secret stair,
that Thou mayst answer all
    my need—
yea, every bygone prayer.

The Darling of the World

Robert Herrick

The darling of the world is come,
and fit it is, we find a room
to welcome Him. The nobler part
of all the house here, is the heart.

Which we will give Him,
    and bequeath
this holly, and this ivy wreath,
to do Him honor, who's our King,
and Lord of all this reveling.

"What means this glory round our feet,"
the Magi mused, "more bright than morn?"
And voices chanted clear and sweet,
"Today the Prince of Peace is born!"

"What means that star," the shepherds said,
"That brightens through the rocky glen?"
And angels, answering overhead,
sang, "Peace on earth, goodwill to men!"

—James Russell Lowell

The adoration of shepherds in stained glass by L. Balmet, Notre Dame de Lellis in Annec, France. Image © Renáta Sedmáková/Adobe Stock

The Annunciation and Nativity

Luke 1:26–33; 2:1–7

And in the sixth month the angel Gabriel was sent from God unto a city of Galilee, named Nazareth, To a virgin espoused to a man whose name was Joseph, of the house of David; and the virgin's name was Mary. And the angel came in unto her, and said, Hail, thou that art highly favoured, the Lord is with thee: blessed art thou among women.

And when she saw him, she was troubled at his saying, and cast in her mind what manner of salutation this should be.

And the angel said unto her, Fear not, Mary: for thou hast found favour with God. And, behold, thou shalt conceive in thy womb, and bring forth a son, and shalt call his name Jesus. He shall be great, and shall be called the Son of the Highest: and the Lord God shall give unto him the throne of his father David: And he shall reign over the house of Jacob for ever; and of his kingdom there shall be no end.

■ ■ ■ ■ ■

And it came to pass in those days, that there went out a decree from Caesar Augustus that all the world should be taxed. (And this taxing was first made when Cyrenius was governor of Syria.) And all went to be taxed, every one into his own city. And Joseph also went up from Galilee, out of the city of Nazareth, into Judaea, unto the city of David, which is called Bethlehem; (because he was of the house and lineage of David:) To be taxed with Mary his espoused wife, being great with child.

And so it was, that, while they were there, the days were accomplished that she should be delivered. And she brought forth her first-born son, and wrapped him in swaddling clothes, and laid him in a manger; because there was no room for them in the inn.

Painting by Alan Lathwell. Image © Alan Lathwell/Advocate Art

The Angels and Shepherds

Luke 2:8–20

And there were in the same country shepherds abiding in the field, keeping watch over their flock by night. And, lo, the angel of the Lord came upon them, and the glory of the Lord shone round about them: and they were sore afraid.

And the angel said unto them, Fear not: for, behold, I bring you good tidings of great joy, which shall be to all people. For unto you is born this day in the city of David a Saviour, which is Christ the Lord. And this shall be a sign unto you; Ye shall find the babe wrapped in swaddling clothes, lying in a manger.

And suddenly there was with the angel a multitude of the heavenly host praising God, and saying, Glory to God in the highest, and on earth peace, good will toward men.

And it came to pass, as the angels were gone away from them into heaven, the shepherds said one to another, Let us now go even unto Bethlehem, and see this thing which is come to pass, which the Lord hath made known unto us.

And they came with haste, and found Mary, and Joseph, and the babe lying in a manger. And when they had seen it, they made known abroad the saying which was told them concerning this child. And all they that heard it wondered at those things which were told them by the shepherds. But Mary kept all these things, and pondered them in her heart.

And the shepherds returned, glorifying and praising God for all the things that they had heard and seen, as it was told unto them.

Painting by Alan Lathwell. Image © Alan Lathwell/Advocate Art

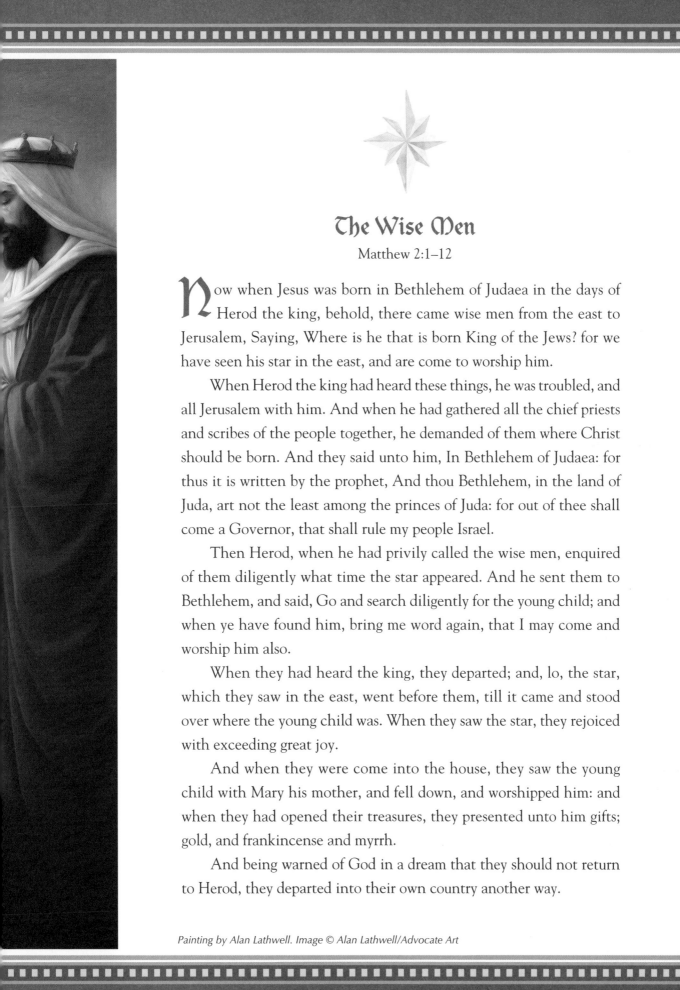

The Wise Men

Matthew 2:1–12

Now when Jesus was born in Bethlehem of Judaea in the days of Herod the king, behold, there came wise men from the east to Jerusalem, Saying, Where is he that is born King of the Jews? for we have seen his star in the east, and are come to worship him.

When Herod the king had heard these things, he was troubled, and all Jerusalem with him. And when he had gathered all the chief priests and scribes of the people together, he demanded of them where Christ should be born. And they said unto him, In Bethlehem of Judaea: for thus it is written by the prophet, And thou Bethlehem, in the land of Juda, art not the least among the princes of Juda: for out of thee shall come a Governor, that shall rule my people Israel.

Then Herod, when he had privily called the wise men, enquired of them diligently what time the star appeared. And he sent them to Bethlehem, and said, Go and search diligently for the young child; and when ye have found him, bring me word again, that I may come and worship him also.

When they had heard the king, they departed; and, lo, the star, which they saw in the east, went before them, till it came and stood over where the young child was. When they saw the star, they rejoiced with exceeding great joy.

And when they were come into the house, they saw the young child with Mary his mother, and fell down, and worshipped him: and when they had opened their treasures, they presented unto him gifts; gold, and frankincense and myrrh.

And being warned of God in a dream that they should not return to Herod, they departed into their own country another way.

The Magi Call Him King: A Christmas Song

Effie Lee Newsome

O shepherds, while
   you watch your flocks
the Wise Men watch His star,
the Magi who come worshiping
with incense from afar.

Know, shepherds, you
   who find the place,
so humble, where He lies,

the Magi ride with splendid gifts
under the midnight skies.

Oh you of sheep,
   who seek the fold
of Him the angels sing,
though He be called
   "Good Shepherd" too,
the Magi call him King.

Fresco in Zurich by Fritz Kunz. Image © sedmak/iStock

The First Christmas

Marian Swinger

It never snows at Christmas in that dry and dusty land.
Instead of freezing blizzards, there are palms and drifting sands,
and years ago a stable and a most unusual star
and three Wise Men who followed it, by camel, not by car,
while, sleepy on the quiet hills, a shepherd gave a cry.
He'd seen a crowd of angels in the silent starlit sky.
In the stable, ox and ass stood very still and calm
and gazed upon the baby, safe and snug in Mary's arms.
And Joseph, lost in shadows, face lit by an oil lamp's glow
stood wondering, that first Christmas Day, two thousand years ago.

Christmas Eve

Christina G. Rossetti

Christmas hath a darkness
brighter than the blazing noon;
Christmas hath a chillness
warmer than the heat of June;
Christmas hath a beauty
lovelier than the world can show:
for Christmas bringeth Jesus,
brought for us so low.

Earth, strike up your music,
birds that sing and bells that ring;
Heaven hath answering music
for all angels soon to sing.
Earth, put on your whitest
bridal robe of spotless snow:
for Christmas bringeth Jesus,
brought for us so low.

Moonless Darkness Stands Between

Gerard Manley Hopkins

Moonless darkness stands between.
Past, O Past, no more be seen!
But the Bethlehem star may lead me
to the sight of Him who freed me
from the self that I have been.
Make me pure, Lord: Thou art holy;
Make me meek, Lord: Thou wert lowly;
now beginning, and alway:
now begin, on Christmas Day.

FROM Music on Christmas Morning

Anne Brontë

Music I love—but never strain
could kindle raptures so divine,
so grief assuage, so conquer pain,
and rouse this pensive heart of mine—
as that we hear on Christmas morn,
upon the wintry breezes borne.

Though Darkness still her empire keep,
and hours must pass, ere morning break;
from troubled dreams, or slumbers deep,
that music kindly bids us wake:
it calls us, with an angel's voice,
to wake, and worship, and rejoice;

to greet with joy the glorious morn,
which angels welcomed long ago,
when our redeeming Lord was born,
to bring the light of Heaven below.

A Christmas Wish for You
Eileen Spinelli

Oh, may the Christmas angel fly to your home
while you are sleeping.
May she decorate your rooftop with stars.
May she stir the fire in your hearth
and bring warmth to your rooms
and to your heart.
Softly may she make her way into your kitchen,
tie your flowered apron around her waist.
May she sprinkle the cookies you baked
with a confetti of laughter,
ladle peace into your favorite blue bowls,
sweep the dust of old griefs out the back door.
Oh, may the Christmas angel breathe love
into every corner,
and sweeten your dreams with hope
this blessed silent night.

Sing a Song of Christmas
Gail Brook Burket

Sing a song of Christmas—
of starlight on the snow,
of scarlet flames of
    Yuletide logs
and candles' golden glow.

Sing a song of Christmas—
of mistletoe and pine,

of holly wreaths and
    balsam trees
whose lights and tinsel shine.

Sing a song of Christmas—
of bells which gaily ring,
and carols on the frosty air
the strolling minstrels sing.

Sing a song of Christmas—
of happiness and cheer,
and love which lights the
    earth with joy
to bless the coming year.

Image © GAP Interiors/The CONTENTed Nest

Giving

James E. Feig

May all your gifts at Christmas be
bright packages beneath your tree,
filled with blessings from above
and cheerful smiles from those you love;
filled with happiness untold,
lasting friendships, new and old;
peace and joy, contentment, too,
enough to last the whole
year through.

ISBN: 978-1-5460-0675-6

Published by Ideals
Hachette Book Group
1290 Avenue of the Americas
New York, NY 10104

Printed and bound in Canada • FRI

Publisher, Peggy Schaefer
Editor, Melinda Rathjen
Designer and Photo Research, Marisa Jackson
Proofreader, Rebekah Moredock

Cover: Daniel Rodgers/Advocate Art
Inside front cover art: *North Pole* by Jenny Newland. Image © Jenny Newland/Art Licensing
Inside back cover art: *Under the Christmas Tree* by Janet Pidoux. Image © Janet Pidoux/Art Licensing
Additional art credits: "Bits & Pieces" artwork by Emily van Wyk

Join a community of *Ideals* readers on Facebook at: www.facebook.com/IdealsMagazine

ACKNOWLEDGMENTS

FIELD, RACHEL. "Snow in the City." Excerpted from *POEMS* by Rachel Field. Poem Copyright © 1934 MPC; 1962 Arthur S. Pederson. Reprinted with the permission of Simon & Schuster Books for Young Readers, an imprint of Simon & Schuster Children's Publishing Division. All rights reserved. GIRANDO, JAN MILLER. "Don't Waste the Miracle." Originally published in *Believe: A Christmas Treasury* by Mary Engelbreit, © 1998 by Mary Engelbreit Ink, published by Andrews McMeel Publishing. HOLMES, MARJORIE. "Sing a Song of Christmas Carols" from *At Christmas the Heart Goes Home* by Marjorie Holmes. Copyright © 1991 by Marjorie Holmes. Used by permission of the author. HUGHES, LANGSTON. "Christmas Eve: Nearing Midnight in New York" from *The Collected Poems of Langston Hughes* by Langston Hughes, edited by Arnold Rampersad with David Roessel, Associate Editor, copyright © 1994 by the Estate of Langston Hughes. Used by permission of Alfred A. Knopf, an imprint of the Knopf Doubleday Publishing Group, a division of Penguin Random House LLC. All rights reserved. MCGINLEY, PHYLLIS. "Lady Selecting Her Christmas Card" copyright © 1960 by Phyllis McGinley. Currently published in *Times Three*, originally published by Viking. Reprinted by permission of Curtis Brown, Ltd. OUR THANKS to the following authors or their heirs for permission granted or for material submitted for publication: Bea Bourgeois, Anne Kennedy Brady, Iris W. Bray, Gail Brook Burket, Michele Christian, Lansing Christman, Helen Crawford, James E. Feig, Elsie Melchert Fowler, Marguerite Gode, Charles R. Isley, Minnie Klemme, Pamela Kennedy, Karen Lee, Andrew Luna, Letitia Morse Nash, Fritz Peters, Garnett Ann Schultz, Helen C. Smith, Eileen Spinelli, Alice Mackenzie Swaim, and Marian Swinger. Scripture quotations are taken from the King James Version (KJV).

Every effort has been made to establish ownership and use of each selection in this book. If contacted, the publisher will be pleased to rectify any errors or omissions in subsequent editions.